FORAGING

THE ULTIMATE BEGINNER'S GUIDE TO FORAGING WILD EDIBLE PLANTS & MEDICINAL HERBS

By Jerry Langford

CONTENTS

INTRODUCTION

Many people think that in case of a catastrophe, they will turn into a great hunter if they find themselves stranded in the wilderness. We have seen shows on Discovery and Hollywood movies, which shows a Tom Dick Harry getting lost and forced to survive in nature. Fast forward to Tom sitting near a fire, roasting a large animal, and you just realize you have entered into a fantasy world.

However, let me break it out to you – it doesn't work like that. Quite frankly, hunting in the wilderness is hard when you do not have the weapon or the right skill. Hunting also takes a great deal of energy and instincts. You may take days to find and harvest an animal or plant. You will need endurance and in the wilderness, edible plants will help you fuel your energy.

Dining on edible plants is the right way to keep your body going when you are without your regular source of food. Did you know that you could eat weeds and get the required nutrition for your body to keep moving? You will probably not feel full after eating loads of weeds but you will be able to sustain for long enough to find your way for help or to scavenge for an animal.

This book will guide you with the basics of foraging. You will read about the most common edibles found growing in the wild. This book is a stepping stone with a small sampling; there are literally hundreds of plants, trees, and bushes that are safe to eat. Foraging requires time and great deal of practice. Once you finish reading this book, you must get out and give it a shot. Study some plants, eat it, and you will get an idea what to do during an emergency. Remember, do not panic and stay calm – that's the key to foraging.

Happy foraging!

CHAPTER 1: AN INTRODUCTION TO FORAGING

At its most basic level, foraging is simply searching for wild resources. In most cases, foraging applies to searching for wild edibles like berries, roots, and weeds. Countless animal species subsist on foods they find from foraging and people too can gather some valuable resources from the wild if you know where to look. Things that look like weeds (and may in fact BE weeds) could actually be edible foods that you can serve for dinner! Everything from wild mushrooms, berries, leaves, and roots can be eaten as long as you gather the right species and clean them properly.

Basic Rules for Foraging

When it comes to foraging, there are certain rules you should be prepared to follow. Some of these rules are designed for your own safety – you must realize that certain plants are poisonous and you need to learn which ones they are. Other rules are based in etiquette – you should not "forage" in your neighbor's garden, for example. In the following pages you will find lists of rules to help you become the best forager you can possibly be. Make sure you read and familiarize yourself with all of these rules before you go out foraging on your own.

Quick-Start Guide to Foraging

Becoming an expert forager is not something you can do overnight. You need to take your time in learning how to identify edible plants and then check and double check your identification to make sure you are correct. The last thing you want to do is rush out to collect some wild edibles and end up bringing home a basket full of toxic look-alikes. The more care you take in learning the proper rules to follow when foraging, the better off you will be. To give you an idea what it will take to become a forager, consider the quick-start guide below.

<u>Below you will find a list of steps to follow to become a forager</u>:

Invest in a high-quality plant guide book – you want something with plenty of information, tips for identification, and pictures. Some good guide books to consider include:
Stalking the Wild Asparagus, Euell Gibbons

The Wild Foot Trail Guide, Alan Hall
The Forager's Harvest, Samuel Thayer

Purchase other foraging gear like hiking boots, long pants (to avoid poison ivy), gardening gloves, pruning shears (kitchen shears will work too), and a spade.
Choose a basket or bag that you will carry with you to harvest your edibles – you'll also want a collection of sandwich bags to keep your plants separated.

Practice identifying plants in your backyard and in local parks – try to identify them without the guide book then check yourself.

Keep practicing – do not go out foraging for real (and definitely don't eat anything you gather) until you are absolutely certain you are ready.

Start off small – on your first forage, gather just a few plants that you are absolutely sure you have identified correctly.

Go through the proper procedure to test your plants, making sure they are safe to consume.

Expand your horizons – as you gain more experience with foraging you can increase the number of different plants you harvest (just be sure to test them all).

Remember, foraging for wild edibles can be dangerous if you make a mistake in identification. Do not rush yourself when you are just starting out.

The longer you take to familiarize yourself with edible plants, the better.

Safety Rules for Foraging

Foraging can be a fun learning experience, but it can also be very dangerous if you make a mistake in identifying a plant. <u>Below you will find a collection of safety rules to follow when foraging on your own</u>:

Learn to identify different kinds of poisonous plants you are likely to encounter during foraging – know what they look like and how to identify them.

Always identify your edibles by their Botanical name – especially when sharing information with other foragers – some plants have different English and Botanical names.

Do not gather (or eat) anything that you cannot positively identify – if you aren't absolutely sure that it is safe, do not eat it!

Always cross-reference your edibles before you eat them to be completely sure they are safe – many plants have toxic look-alikes that can easily fool you.

Do not forage for edibles in places that are likely to be contaminated by pollution, pesticides, fertilizers, etc.

Always clean your edibles properly before you eat them – rinse them well each and every time.

Test your edibles in small amounts – ideally you should test one plant at a time, one new plant a day, to see how your body reacts.

Etiquette and Common Sense Rules for Foraging

In addition to learning the safety rules from the last section you also need to pay attention to some etiquette and common sense rules for foraging. These rules will help you to get the most out of your foraging while being respectful of other foragers and the environment.

Familiarize yourself with the plants that are endangered in your area and do not pick them – it may even be illegal to do so.

Only pick as much as you need of any given plant and never take all of a plant in a certain patch – you want to leave some to grow.

Be very careful when harvesting roots from a plant – if you damage the roots you could kill the entire plant.

Do not forage in nature reserves – these areas exist to preserve plant and animal species.

Spread some seeds once in a while – it is especially important to sow seeds for native species.

Always clean up after yourself when you are out foraging – never leave any litter behind.

Make sure the edibles you are harvesting are in fact wild – do not take plants from anyone's property.

Chapter 2: Top 10 Edible Plants Found in the Wild

There are hundreds of things to dine upon in the wild. These top 10 are the most common. Every region will have its own native plants and trees. It is a good idea to brush up on those that are most likely to be in your region.

Dandelions

Dandelions are probably one of the most recognizable plants on the planet. They are considered an obnoxious weed to most who work hard to eradicate the dandelions at the first sign of the yellow flowers in their lawn.

Dandelions are actually a common edible with many people in the southern states regularly eating the plants. The flowers themselves can be eaten raw or sauteed and tossed on a bed of greens. The leaves are edible, but they do have a slightly bitter taste. The leaves are best enjoyed before the flower bud opens. Once the yellow flower is evident, the leaves become much bitter. The stems are edible. The roots can be eaten, but they are not exactly tasty. Dandelion roots are more for medicinal use if you are struggling with constipation. They are very high in fiber and can help relieve those issues.

Dandelions are rich in vitamin A and C. Surprisingly, dandelions also contain more vitamin K than carrots. Dandelions are also rich in calcium and iron, two things that are absolutely necessary for healthy bones and muscles. The plant is also a diuretic, which can help clean your liver and kidney of toxins.

Purslane

If you have a vegetable garden, you have probably dealt with an invasion of purslane. This spreading plant will quickly cover ground that has been disturbed. It is one of the most irritating weeds a gardener will ever face. However, it is actually not a weed and could be added to salad greens. The plump, small leaves hold a great deal of Omega-3 fatty acids. Yes, those are the healthy ones that people often take supplements for. The purslane can be eaten raw, leaves, stems and flowers or cooked up with some other greens for a nice stir-fry of sorts.

Purslane is also high in vitamins E and C. By eating this plant, you are helping your heart, your immune system and your skin. It has a bit of an unexpected citrus flavor that is different and often welcome when you are dining on rather bland greens. Older plants will have a small flower, which is also edible. Ideally, you want to go for the young, oar-shaped leaves. These taste the best. They will have a slight shine to them that helps make them easy to spot in a field of green plants.

Pine Needles

Pine trees are pretty common in any mountainous region. They are not specific to the east or west coasts. The prolific trees are easily identifiable and known for their massive height, long, pokey needles and the traditional pine cone. What many people don't know about the pine tree is it can actually provide a great deal of nutrition if you know where to look.

Green pine needles collected from a live branch can be put into a pot of water and heated over a fire. This creates something known as pine needle tea. Pine needle tea is absolutely packed with vitamin C. If you are in a survival situation, you need your immune system to remain strong. Boosts of vitamin C will help do just that. The tea is actually a remedy for congestion as well if you happen to have a stuffed up nose or a cough.

The tea is actually not bad tasting either. It can be a bit sharp, but you can certainly dilute it if it is too strong for you. If you are caught in the cold, drinking a cup of hot pine needle tea will help warm you from the inside while providing you some needed nutrition.

You can also use spruce tree needles that have similar qualities.

Pine Nuts

There is a reason squirrels hang out in pine trees; they are going after the pine nuts. Yes, pine nuts, those little nuts you buy in the store that cost a small fortune, are right there in the pine cones. Pine nuts are absolutely delicious and contain a great deal of protein and iron. These are things that are hard to come by when you are foraging plants and are typically found in meat.

The only real drawback with pine nuts is getting the little things. There is a reason they cost a lot at the grocery store. The tiny nuts are embedded in the pine cones behind the sharp outer edges. You will want to use a stick or knife to peel back the layers to reach the nuts. In most cases, you are going to have to pick pine cones from the tree in order to get the nuts. The pine cones lying on the ground are likely already going to be picked clean of nuts by the local squirrels.

Pine nuts do take a lot of work to get, but they are so good. You can heat them or eat them raw. Toss them in your salad made of up edibles for a nice crunch.

Cattails

If you stumble upon a swamp or marsh area, you are likely to find cattails. If you find cattails, consider yourself very fortunate. These plants are at the top of the foraging list. They are good to eat and have many uses in a survival situation in general. Cattails are the cat's meow!

The root of the cattail is the most sought after. Peel back the outer layer and munch on the crunchy center. If you are planning on staying out in the wild for long, you can dry and grind the root into a powder to make biscuits or flatbread. It is very high in starch. Heating the root over an open fire until it is slightly black is another way to eat it. Do not eat the stringy, fiber-like parts of the root.

The seed head at the top of the stalk can be eaten in the late summer. This is the part of the plant that will turn brown in the fall. Simply toss the seed heads into a pot of water or heat over an open fire and eat as you would corn on the cob. It is actually quite tasty and one of the reasons survivalists get excited when they find a stand of cattails.

There are not a lot of vitamins and minerals in the cattail, but it is still a valuable addition to any foraging diet.

White Mustard

This is another "weed" you will find growing on hillsides, along roadways and pretty much all over the place. It is called white mustard because of its pale stems; however, the flowers are yellow. The entire plant is edible, but people tend to love the bold taste of the flowers. They have a bit of a peppery taste, which make them a welcome addition to any salad.

As the flowers age, they turn to seed. Mustard seed is a common addition to recipes in the kitchen, but you can eat them raw as well. The seeds can be ground up and added to that starchy powder you collected from the cattail roots to create a flavored biscuit.

Mustard seeds are actually pretty high in calories, which may not be good today, but in a survival situation, that is a very good thing. You want to eat lots of calories in order to keep your energy up. Adding mustard seeds to your dandelion salad will give you a nice, well-rounded meal, packed with calories. Mustard seeds also have a lot of B vitamins, which are turned into energy.

Wild Asparagus

If you happen to find this little gem growing alongside a roadway, you are in luck. Wild asparagus looks very similar to the stuff you buy in the grocery store. It is a little skinnier and the top portion that is usually the thick, tasty stuff is a little thinner and resembles grain. You have to look very close in the weeds to see it. It is easily hidden by other more prolific weeds. It has a feathery appearance at the top. You may also be able to find alongside the fences of farms and along riverbeds.

Asparagus is rich in potassium and vitamins B6 and C. You can steam it over a fire, boil it in a stew or eat it raw. It tastes pretty much the same as the stuff you buy in the stores. When you find it, harvest it about an inch off the ground. Use a knife to cut the stalk. Pay close attention to the area where you found the first bit; you are likely to see more if you are looking carefully. Asparagus is found in the early to late spring in most parts of the country.

Kelp

It certainly doesn't look appealing floating in lakes and rivers, but is a food that can help sustain you. If you are in survival mode, you have probably found a source of water. The kelp is basically brown seaweed. The thick, ribbon like seaweed may be floating just below the surface and reach all the way to the bottom of the body of water. It thrives on sunlight, which means it is rich in vitamin C. It is also rich in vitamin K and iron. These are some important vitamins and minerals you need to stay healthy and strong.

The kelp can be eaten raw or cooked. As you can imagine, it is slimy, which may be a little tough for some to eat in raw form. You could also dry some kelp in the sun, on a rock, grind it up and use it to flavor a tossed salad made with other edible plants you collected. It can take the place of salt if you need a little kick to your meal.

There are numerous varieties of kelp, but all are edible. One of the best things about kelp is you can find it year round. In the dead of winter when plant life is tough to come by, you can always fall back on kelp. With that said, use a stick or something to pull it out of the water. You don't want to get cold and risk hypothermia.

Nuts

If you come across any kind of nut trees in your travels, you are in luck. Nuts are high in protein, taste delicious and can help keep you going. However, most nut trees are going to be found growing in warmer climates, like the south or sunny California. If you are in one of those warm areas, look for nut trees.

Things like walnuts, acorns, hazelnuts and even peanuts are excellent additions to your foraging diet. Keep in mind, some nut trees are extremely tall. Harvesting nuts can be a real chore and if it isn't safe to climb, avoid going after the nuts. You can't risk breaking a bone or suffering an injury due to falling out of a tree.

Peanuts are an excellent option because they do not grow in huge trees. Peanuts are actually a root crop! You need to get familiar with the peanut plant so you can pull it and harvest the tasty nuts that are growing in the dirt. A single peanut plant can grow about 30 to 40 pods. This is good eating for anybody tired of eating dandelions and other leaves.

The peanut plant resembles a pea plant, but produces yellow flowers in the spring. The stalks will bury themselves in the ground and that is where the peanuts are formed. The pods are ready to harvest in the fall. Peanuts require a lot of heat, which means if you are in the north, you are not likely to find peanuts growing in the wild.

Fireweed

This is a common weed found across the United States, but hot areas like Texas and the deep south may not be so lucky to find this weed growing in the wild. The name fireweed was given to the tall plant because it is usually the first thing to start growing on land that has been ravished by fire. It is easy to spot and will cover an area with an array of bright, pink flowers. It grows anywhere from 3 to 6 feet tall. If you are on a hill, you will be able to spot a field of fireweed pretty easily.

It is rich in vitamins A and C and is often used medicinally to treat colds. The flowers produce a sweet honey substance that is a real treat for the person surviving on bitter leaves and flowers. The shoots of the plant are best consumed when they are young. They will have a bit of an asparagus taste. The older shoots will be very tough. The flowers tend to have a little kick to them, which some have compared to a pepper taste.

CHAPTER 3: TOP 7 MEDICINAL PLANTS FOUND IN THE WILD

Medicinal plants have been used for centuries. They have lost favor in the modern world, but there are still plenty of people who have had the knowledge passed down to them from past generations. In some cases, scientific studies have actually been done to determine the validity of some of the "old folk remedies" and not surprising, those remedies were proven to be legit.

Medicinal plants are typically used in three different ways.

Poultices—A poultice is made by grinding up the medicinal plant to form a paste. In some cases, you may want to combine a few plants to create the perfect poultice. You can use a mortar and pestle, your hands or a rock to make a poultice.

Teas—Teas are made by heating the portion of the medicinal plant that you need in water. Teas are also used to make compresses. Soaking a cloth in the tea and then applying externally is an option.

Raw (ingested)—It is rare, but in some cases eating the raw form of a medicinal plant is necessary. Usually, raw is left for topical applications. Ingesting a medicinal plant is rarely called for.

Shepherd's Purse

This pesky weed is typically found growing in dry, rocky soils. It resembles the dandelion leaves on the bottom of the plant as it fans out in a circular pattern. The distinctive tall stalk with heart-shaped seed pods will help you identify this plant.

The leaves of the plant can be used to make a tea. Drinking the tea will help minimize internal bleeding. It is also useful in treating diarrhea and dysentery. Those that have high blood pressure can drink the tea to help reduce blood pressure. A poultice made from the ground leaves can be applied to bleeding wounds to stop the bleeding.

Shepard's Purse is also a common edible that is tossed into salads. You can toss it into a soup or stew as well. The roots can be dried and used as a ginger substitute if you were looking for something a little spicy to add to your stews in the wild.

Mullein

This weed has some pretty unique qualities that set it apart from any other medicinal plant. It is quite tall, in some cases reaching as high as 8 feet. The sage green plant has large leaves on the bottom that narrow as it gets taller. The seed head is bar-like and when it is in bloom, yellow flowers cover the length of the seed head. If you still are not sure, rubbing your hand across one of the leaves will tell you it is mullein. The leaves are incredibly soft, similar to velvet.

Speaking of those super soft leaves, when nature calls, you will be most appreciative to have a few mullein leaves on hand! You will find mullein plants growing along highways and rocky roadways. They thrive in full sun and are drought tolerant.

You can use the leaves to wrap a wound. Antiseptic qualities will help relieve some of the pain while protecting it from getting dirty. Boiling the leaves to make a tea is a common medicine used to treat chest congestion. The flower can be used to make a tea. Soak a piece of cloth in the tea and apply to an earache. Ideally, an infused oil would be made with the mullein flowers, but in a survival situation, you are not likely to have any olive oil around. The compress will work, but isn't as effective as the oil directly into the ear.

Echinacea

Echinacea is often referred to as the purple coneflower. The flower has become quite popular in the home garden because it isn't only beautiful, but because it attracts butterflies and has medicinal properties. The purple flower blooms throughout the summer months and can handle dry spells.

Echinacea is commonly used today for its immune-boosting properties. Drinking a tea infused with the echinacea flowers at the first sign of a cold will help shorten the illness or hold it at bay altogether. The leaves have anti-fungal properties. Drinking an echinacea tea will help promote healing while battling infection in an open wound.

The echinacea can also be made into a poultice and applied directly to spider bites and snake bites. Ideally, you would want to apply externally while still taking internally to give your body the best shot at fighting off infection and a loss of tissue that is common with venomous bites.

Lavender

Lavender is a common plant found in many people's landscaping. It also grows wild on hillsides. The unique lavender smell is one way to identify the plant. The other way is the pretty purple flowers that bloom along the stalk of the plant. The leaves are a pale green and from a distance may look grey.

Lavender is a very desirable plant to come upon in the wild. The smell from the flowers alone will help to calm your nerves. Grinding the flowers into a poultice and applying to sunburns, rashes and bug bites will provide almost immediate relief while promoting healing. Brewing a lavender tea is another way to treat wounds by soaking a cloth in the tea and then applying to a wound. The antiseptic properties help promote healing while providing pain relief.

Drinking lavender tea will help calm and relax you if you are overly stressed. It is also helpful in solving some digestive issues, like an upset stomach. Wiping a fussy baby down with a lavender soaked cloth can help calm the child.

Plantain

The plantain is another plant that is considered a weed. It thrives in warm, dry and rocky areas. The deep green leaves are low growing and have a ridged appearance. The leaves tend to be about as large as your palm. The plantain leaf is another common substitute for toilet paper in an emergency.

It is mainly used externally in either a poultice or a tea is brewed to make a compress. The plantain is a very versatile plant. It can be used to treat bug bites, bee stings, soothe a rash, burns and sun burns and the list goes on. You can use a plantain poultice to stop a wound from bleeding.

The leaves can be made into a tea. The tea can be drunk and used as a diuretic if the kidneys are having problems. It has also been used to treat lung infections. If you have athletes foot, a plantain poultice or a compress with plantain tea can help stop the burning while clearing up the fungus.

Burdock

The burdock plant is a little intimidating with little green hairs sticking out of the purple flower, but they are not bad. It resembles the thistle that will poke you. It will only grow in rocky areas and areas where there is plenty of sun exposure. You won't find it in the forest or a heavily treed or shaded area. It is one of those weeds that can be found growing alongside highways mixed in with the mullein.

The burdock leaves can be applied directly to bites, stings and burns for immediate relief. Brewing the leaves into a tea provides an excellent remedy for cold symptoms. It is also a natural diuretic. Grinding the leaves, flowers and roots into a poultice is a good treatment for open wounds. The antibacterial qualities will help stave off infection and promote healing.

Burdock leaves are also an excellent option for wrapping up any meat you may harvest. The leaves can be used to create a boat, similar to an aluminum foil boat you would use to cook veggies and meat. Place the wrapped food on the hot rocks of your fire or in the coals.

Kudzu

This plant is a lucky find, but you will only find it in the south eastern states. It was actually planted in the areas on purpose to help control erosion, but now it is considered to be a nuisance and is regularly sprayed with weed killer. It is a prolific plant, which is bad for landscape, but excellent for someone fighting to survive. To give you an idea of the growth of kudzu, it can grow 7 feet in a single week. Many states ban the introduction of kudzu into their lands.

Each part of the kudzu plant can be eaten raw or cooked. However, it is an excellent remedy for headaches and migraines. It is a natural anti-inflammatory. Arthritis pain, sprains and strains will all feel better with an infusion of kudzu tea. Something that some folks don't want to think about or talk about is withdrawals from alcohol should one find themselves stranded. Alcohol withdrawals can be pretty severe for alcoholics. The root of the kudzu can be dried and ground up to form a powder. Eat the powder or mix up in a cup of water. The kudzu root will help eliminate the desire for alcohol and help control the withdrawal symptoms. The plant will also help the liver restore itself and the person suffering alcoholism will feel better in general.

CHAPTER 4: GROWING PLANTS IN YOUR GARDEN

Growing your own medicinal plants is super easy. There are numerous herbs that are quite prolific and easy to grow in a kitchen window, on your deck or in your garden. While herbs tend to be fairly inexpensive, growing your own fresh herbs is a better option. Fresh or raw herbs hold more medicinal value than dried herbs. However, for long term storage, you will need to dry your herbs. In fact, they are so prolific, you will need to dry them once they start producing.

These herbs can be used to spice up recipes or medicinally.

Peppermint

Peppermint is a very aromatic herb that can be used to treat numerous ailments. If you have a headache, smelling peppermint leaves will help alleviate it. You can dry the leaves and use them to make a tea. The tea is an excellent tonic to treat an upset stomach along with stomach cramps. Peppermint is invigorating. Keeping dried leaves around can help energize you and your mind.

Garlic

Garlic is an easy plant to grow all year around. Garlic is nature's answer to antibiotics. If you are dealing with an infection or want to prevent an infection, adding fresh garlic to your meals is one way to do that. You can also dry the garlic and drink it in a tea, although it does tend to be very strong and isn't always appealing. Roasting the garlic and eating it that way is another way to get it in your system. Garlic is also an excellent way to treat high blood pressure, can lower bad cholesterol levels and can help manage Type 2 diabetes. It is one of those super plants you definitely want to have in your garden.

Aloe Vera

Aloe Vera is a very common houseplant as well as a desirable addition to many skin lotions. Aloe is easy to grow and will thrive with very little care. The aloe plant contains liquid in each of the stalks. Cut off a piece of the plant and squeeze the juice onto a wound to help promote healing. The aloe vera juice can also be used to ease the pain of a burn or bug bite. Aloe can also be taken internally. It will help boost the immune system while healing the digestive system. Drinking a couple ounces of aloe vera before a meal can combat heartburn.

Sage

Sage is a common spice used in the kitchen and it is an excellent way to flavor stews and casseroles. It is also an excellent remedy for sore throats and colds. A sage tea is an excellent way to relieve the pain of a sore throat. It will also help relieve a cough and the sniffles that accompany a cold. Sage is an astringent and can be used as a mouthwash as well. When you are working hard to survive and getting a little sweaty and stinky, rubbing a bit of sage under your armpits will reduce the odor.

Thyme

Thyme isn't just for roasted meat. It is an excellent remedy for sores on the skin and skin rashes. A poultice made of ground thyme should be applied to the afflicted area sparingly. It is a good idea to mix the thyme with vodka or vinegar. Thyme is very powerful. A teaspoon of dried leaves in a cup of hot water can be used to treat bronchitis. Drink the tea once a day. If you are dealing with insects invading your camp, burn thyme to keep them at bay. Insect bites can result in disease or open wounds from excessive scratching. Rinsing the mouth with a tea made with thyme leaves can help stop an infection and prevent further pain in the gums and teeth.

Ginger

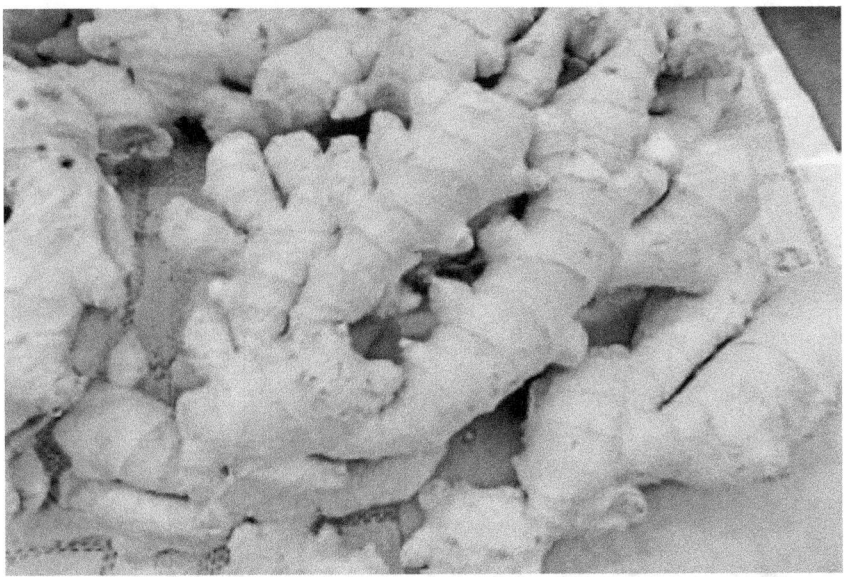

Ginger is the life's answer to any kind of stomach or gastrointestinal issue. Whether you have vomiting, diarrhea, cramping, bloating or icky in general, ginger can make it better. Foraging and living off the land can result in stomach upset from eating new foods or drinking tainted water. Ginger can help resolve those symptoms. You can make a ginger tea, which is a very pleasant drink. You can also use the ginger to flavor a soup or stew. Chewing on a piece of raw ginger root is also effective.

Cayenne Pepper

Cayenne pepper may not appeal to most, but it is something you definitely want to have around in case of emergencies. Cayenne pepper should be added to any first aid kit. You can grow your own peppers and dry them to make cayenne pepper at home. Cayenne pepper can stop bleeding. Taken internally, it can stop internal bleeding or used to place directly on open wounds that won't stop bleeding. Oddly enough, cayenne pepper can also be drank as a tea to open up blood vessels if you suspect you are having a heart attack or a stroke. It is taken on a regular basis to help relieve sinus pressure and other side effects of the common cold. Add a couple teaspoons to a cup of hot water and gargling with it will help soothe a sore throat while healing any blisters that may be inside the mouth and throat area. Cayenne pepper is truly one of the most important plants you should have in your kitchen garden.

CHAPTER 5: PLANTS TO BE AVOIDED

While there are plenty of plants in the wild that can be safely eaten, there are plenty of plants that should be avoided. Many edible plants have very similar looking "brothers" growing in the wild that are actually toxic. It can be difficult to tell good plants from bad plants. There are some key signs you should look for before you decide to eat a plant or take the plant edibility test (explained in next section).

The following characteristics may be present in an edible plant as well as a poisonous one. However, a plant that is safe to eat will likely have only 1 of these characteristics while an unsafe plant would have several. If you are unsure, always use the plant edibility test or move on to something you are sure about.

- Plants that have thorns, stickers or sharp pokes
- Plants that have a milky substance inside the stem
- Plants that are excessively bitter (however, many edibles do have a bitter taste)
- Foliage that resembles parsnip or carrots

- A strong almond scent to the leaves or stems
- Seed heads that have purple, black or pink spurs
- Leaves that grow in 3s, think poison ivy
- Shiny leaves
- Soapy taste
- Seed pods on the plant—beans in your garden are fine, anything growing in the wild that resembles a bean or pea is not

The following are a couple little sayings that have been passed down through the ages to try and help people remember what is safe and what isn't.

- Leaves of three, stay away from me.
- For berries—Red could be dead
- Black and blue, good for you
- White and yellow could kill a fellow

Mushrooms and berries may seem like a good idea, but they are rarely safe to eat unless you know exactly what it is you are picking. About half the red berries found in the wild are safe to eat. One way to get an idea of what berries are safe is by looking at the birds. Are the birds eating the berries? If not, they are not safe and you should avoid them as well. Mushrooms are a risky business. Unless you are experienced in picking mushrooms and know exactly what to look for, pass on them. You will likely see quite a bit, especially if you are in a forest area, but stay away from them.

It is always best to be safe than sorry. You can technically go 21 days without food. Don't eat mushrooms on day 3 just because you think that is all you will find. The toxins in some plants, berries and mushrooms can make you miserable or even result in death. It is truly not worth the cost of having a little something in your belly.

CHAPTER 6: PLANT EDIBILITY TEST

If you are unsure of a plant's edibility, the universal plant edibility test will help you determine if you can eat a plant. There are some plants that are okay to eat raw and others that must be cooked. Some plants you can eat the leaves, but not the flowers. It is a lot of information to try and retain. If you are going to be surviving in the wild for a long time, you will want to diversify your diet. To do that, you are going to need to test new plants from time to time.
Before starting the test, do not eat anything. Your stomach needs to be empty. You don't want to confuse your reaction to the plant you are testing with what you ate for breakfast. Do not eat the plant again for 24 hours, just to make sure it is not going to result in any negative reactions.

1. Separate the plant into the four main components; roots, stem, leaves, flower
2. Decide what portion of the plant you want to test- Only test one portion at a time.
3. Rub a portion of the plant on the inside of your wrist. Wait 15 to 30 minutes. If there is any redness, burning or itching, the plant isn't safe to eat. If there is no reaction, go on to the next step.

4. Rub another piece of the same portion of the plant around your lips. Wait again. If no signs of an allergic reaction, go on to the next step.

5. Place a small amount of the plant on your tongue. Leave it there for 15 minutes. If you feel burning, swelling or any other adverse reaction, spit it out and look for something else to eat. If there are no side effects, keep going.

6. Eat a small portion of the plant. Pay attention to any gastrointestinal upset over the next 8 hours. If nothing has happened, the plant is likely safe to eat.

Do not get carried away and gorge on any one plant. Even if it is safe to eat, you will likely experience some negative side effects from eating too much of any single plant. Mix it up a bit.

CHAPTER 7: HARVESTING FOOD FOR FORAGING

Now that you know the basic rules for foraging you should learn when the best time is to harvest your edibles. Just as you would plan your harvest for a vegetable garden you keep in your backyard, so should you plan when you will harvest the foods for which you are foraging. It is best to harvest wild edibles when they are at their peak of freshness – when the oils that produce the aroma and flavor of the plant are at their most potent. The peak of freshness for any given plant will vary – the right time for harvesting a certain plant may also vary depending on how you plan to use it (in a salad versus a cooked dish, for example).

<u>Below you will find a list of tips for harvesting certain wild edibles</u>:

For edible wild weeds, harvest the foliage before the plant flowers for the maximum flavor and nutritional content.

When collecting edible flowers (like chamomile), harvest the flowers just before they reach their maximum size.

When harvesting roots (like chicory or burdock), collect the roots in the fall after the above-ground foliage has faded.

Only harvest from mature plants that have enough foliage to maintain their growth after harvesting – you don't want to kill the plant.

Harvest your edibles in the morning after the early morning dew has dried but before the day heats up.

Harvest flowering edibles after they have produced buds but before the buds actually open for the best flavor.

CHAPTER 8: WEEDS! YOU COULD EAT THEM

Many of the same weeds you would remove from your garden are actually edible. Take for example the dandelion (*Taraxacum officinale*). The leaves and roots of the dandelion plant are rich in vitamin C, potassium, calcium, phosphorus, and various other vitamins and minerals. Not only are they very healthy, but they taste great in a salad! Below you will find a list of edible weeds that you should look for when foraging. Make sure you carry a plant identification guide with you so you can be sure the weed you are looking at is actually the one you think it is.

Alfalfa
Blue Vervain
Borage
Broadleaf Plantain
Bugleweed
Bull Thistle
Burdock
Catnip
Cattail
Chamomile
Chickweed
Chicory
Cleavers
Coltsfoot
Common Yarrow
Creeping Charlie
Daisy Fleabane
Dandelion
Echinacea
Elderberry
Evening Primrose
Field Pennycress
Fireweed
Forget Me Not
Garlic Mustard
Goldenrod
Harebell
Henbit
Herb Robert
Hop Clover
Horehound
Horsetail
Horseweed
Japanese Knotweed

Joe Pye Weed
Knapweed
Knotgrass
Kudzu
Lambs Quarters
Mallow
Marsh Marigold
Milk Thistle
Milkweed
Motherwort
Mullein
New England Aster
Oak Leaf Goosefoot
Partridgeberry
Peppergrass
Pickerelweed
Pigweed
Pineapple Weed
Prickly Pear
Purple Deadnettle
Purslane
Queen Anne's Lace
Red Clover
Rue
Self Heal
Shepherd's Purse
Silverweed
Sow Thistle
Spiderwort
Spotted Dead Nettle
Spring Beauty
St. John's Wort
Stinging Nettle
Sunflower

Supplejack Vine
Sweet Rocket
Sweetfern
Tea Plant
Teasel
Toothwort
Trout Lily
Valerian
Vervain Mallow
Wild Bee Balm
Wild Grape Vine
Wild Violet

CHAPTER 9: FLOWERS ARE EDIBLE TOO!

Many of the wild flowers you see in the wild are not just beautiful – they are also edible. Take for example the Daylily (*Hemerocallis spp.*) – the brightly colored bud and flowers of this plant can add flavor and color to your forage salads. Some flowers even provide health benefits like Echinacea, also known as the purple coneflower. This plant is often used to create medicinal tinctures to ward off colds, strep throat, and even urinary tract infections. <u>Below you will find a list of edible flowers to look for when foraging</u>:

Bugleweed

Chickweed
Chicory
Coltsfoot
Daylily
Echinacea
Forget Me Not
Heartsease
Herb Robert
New England Aster
Red Clover
Rose
Sorrel
Spring Beauty
St. John's Wort
Sunflower
Trout Lily
Tulip

Chapter 10: Edible Mushrooms You Could Eat

Many people who get started in foraging are in it for the mushrooms. There are many different kinds of mushrooms out there and some of them are incredibly tasty. It is important that you realize, however, that some of them are very poisonous. It is not recommended that novice foragers hunt for mushrooms because it is very easy to confuse the non-edible varieties with the edible varieties. If you want to try foraging for mushrooms, invest in a very mushroom field guide – you should also try to meet up with an experienced mushroom forager to tag along on a few trips before you head out by yourself.

Once you are ready to forage for mushrooms, look for the following types:

Beefsteak Polypore
Boletes
Chaga
Chanterelles
Chicken Mushroom
Dryad's Saddle
Hen of the Woods
Morel
Oyster Mushrooms
Puffballs
Shaggy Mane

CHAPTER 11: RECIPES FOR PREPARING WILD EDIBLES

Once you have done the hard work of harvesting your wild edibles you get to reap the rewards! There are many different ways to go about preparing wild edibles and the method you choose will depend on the plant. To get you started you will find a collection of some basic preparation methods to use with wild edibles you gather on your foraging trips.

Recipes

Balsamic Sautéed Wild Greens
Wildflower Salad
Garlic Sautéed Wild Mushrooms
Boiled and Buttered Roots
Refreshing Wild Green Smoothie

Balsamic Sautéed Wild Greens

These balsamic sautéed wild greens are incredibly easy to prepare and they make a delicious side dish. Some great greens to use in this recipe include dandelion greens, nettles, and chickweed.

Servings: 4

Ingredients:

4 cups wild greens
1 to 2 tablespoons cooking fat (butter, bacon fat, etc.)
1 to 2 tablespoons balsamic vinegar
Salt and pepper to taste

Instructions:

Trim any thick stems from your wild greens and rinse them well.

Heat the fat in a large skillet over medium heat until melted.

Add the wild greens, tossing to coat with the melted fat.

Cover the skillet and cook for 3 to 5 minutes until the greens are tender.

Toss the greens with the balsamic vinegar and season with salt and pepper to taste.

Wildflower Salad

Wildflowers can add a dash of color to your favorite spring salad, not to mention a hint of natural sweetness. Some of the best flowers to use in this recipe include nasturtium blossoms, violet petals, and daylily blooms.

Servings: 4

Ingredients:

¼ cup extra-virgin olive oil

Juice from 1 large lemon

2 to 3 teaspoons raw honey

Salt and pepper to taste

2 cups fresh wild greens

2 ½ cups fresh wildflower blossoms and petals

2 tablespoons fresh chopped mint

Instructions:

Whisk together the olive oil, lemon juice, honey, salt and pepper in a small bowl.

Combine the wild greens and blossoms in a salad bowl, tossing with the mint.

Toss in the vinaigrette until well coated and serve immediately.

Garlic Sautéed Wild Mushrooms

Wild mushrooms sautéed in garlic and butter are the perfect side dish for nearly any meal. Keep in mind that mushrooms shrink as they cook so you'll need to gather a lot!

Servings: 4

Ingredients:

½ cup extra-virgin olive oil

2 lbs. wild mushrooms

4 large shallots, sliced thin

¼ cup unsalted butter

Salt and pepper to taste
6 cloves fresh minced garlic

Instructions:
Clean the mushrooms thoroughly with a damp paper towel to remove dirt.
Remove the stems from the mushrooms and discard them.
Slice the mushrooms as needed according to their size.
Heat the oil in a heavy saucepan over low heat.
Add the shallots and cook for 4 to 5 minutes until translucent.
Toss in the mushrooms along with the butter and season with salt and pepper to taste.
Sauté the mushrooms for 7 to 8 minutes until they have released their liquid.
Stir in the garlic and cook for 1 to 2 minutes more.
Remove from heat and toss in the parsley then serve warm.

Boiled and Buttered Roots

You can prepare wild roots in the same way you would carrots or potatoes – just chop them up and boil them. Wild roots taste absolutely delicious with butter or you can be a little adventurous and try them with some bacon fat.
Servings: 4
Ingredients:
1 lbs. fresh wild roots
1 tablespoon unsalted butter
Salt and pepper to taste

Instructions:

Clean the roots well to remove all dirt.

Peel the roots and slice them to the desired thickness.

Bring a pot of salted water to boil then add the chopped roots.

Boil for 6 to 8 minutes until the roots reach the desired level of tenderness.

Drain the roots and place them in a bowl.

Add the butter and give it a minute to melt then toss with salt and pepper to taste. Serve hot.

Refreshing Wild Green Smoothie

Enjoy the health benefits of wild greens in this refreshing green smoothie. Feel free to throw in some spinach or kale to supplement your wild edibles if you don't have enough.

Servings: 1

Ingredients:

1 handful wild dandelion leaves
1 handful wild plantain leaves
1 cup frozen sliced strawberries
1 small frozen banana, peeled and sliced
1 cup water
Ice cubes (optional)

Instructions:

Combine the dandelion and plantain leaves in a high-speed blender.

Add the water and blend on high speed until smooth.

Add in the frozen banana and strawberries and blend for 30 to 60 seconds on high speed.

If needed, add a few ice cubes to thicken the smoothie.

* Pour the smoothie into a glass and enjoy immediately.

Conclusion

If you ever find yourself in a situation where food is scarce, you will always find foraging will come to your rescue. You often ignore plants but little did you know they could save your life. Going to the mall or pharmacy gives you exposure to only a small set of edible plants. But it is time for you to gain some first hand practice. This book has helped you in identifying the right plants for foraging.

You can even use edible plants with your meal and get familiar to them. Developing a positive connection with edible plants will help you in a chaotic situation. It will help you calm down, renew your hopes, and enjoy your meal, even if you are in a dire situation. Learn how to make recipes and tea for medicine.

I hope this book has helped you with the basics of foraging. Now, it is time to go out, plant your herb garden, and start drying those herbs.

Thank you once again for reading my book on foraging. I hope it gave you the right motivation to study and learn more about this topic.

Good luck!
Your Name